an infatuation

Poetry

Cover artwork Gordon Parker

M·Q·P

Not by wisdom do [poets] make what they compose, but by a gift of nature and an inspiration similar to that of the diviners and oracles.

Socrates

from **The Canterbury Tales**
The General Prologue

Whan that April with his showres soote
The droughte of March hath perced to the roote,
And bathed every veine in swich licour,
Of which vertu engendred is the flowr;
Whan Zephyrus eek with his sweete breeth
Inspired hath in every holt and heeth
The tendre croppes, and the yonge sonne
Hath in the Ram his halve cours yronne,
And smale fowles maken melodye
That sleepen al the night with open ye —
So priketh hem Nature in hir corages —
Thanne longen folk to goon on pilgrimages

Geoffrey Chaucer (c. 1343–1400)

from **The Nymph's Reply to the Shepherd**

If all the world and love were young,
And truth in every shepherd's tongue,
These pretty pleasures might me move
To live with thee and be thy love.

Time drives the flocks from field to fold
When rivers rage and rocks grow cold,
And Philomel becometh dumb;
The rest complains of cares to come.

The flowers do fade, and wanton fields
To wayward winter reckoning yields;
A honey tongue, a heart of gall,
Is fancy's spring, but sorrow's fall.

Thy gowns, they shoes, thy beds of roses,
Thy cap, thy kirtle, and thy posies
Soon break, soon wither, soon forgotten–
In folly ripe, in reason rotten.

Sir Walter Raleigh (c. 1552–1618)

A poet is, before anything else, a person who is passionately in love with language.

W H Auden

Hot Sun, Cool Fire

Hot sun, cool fire, tempered with sweet air,
Black shade, fair nurse, shadow my white hair.
Shine, sun; burn, fire; breathe, air and ease me;
Black shade, fair nurse, shroud me and please me.
Shadow, my sweet nurse, keep me from burning;
Make not glad my cause cause of mourning.
   Let not my beauty's fire
   Inflame unstaid desire,
   Nor pierce any bright eye
   That wandereth lightly.

George Peele (1557–1596)

The poets of each generation seldom sing a new song. They turn to themes men always have loved, and sing them in the mode of their times.

Clarence Day

The Passionate Shepherd to His Love

Come live with me and be my love,
And we will all the pleasures prove
That valleys, groves, hills, and fields,
Woods, or steepy mountain yields.

And we will sit upon the rocks,
Seeing the shepherds feed their flocks,
By shallow rivers to whose falls
Melodious birds sing madrigals.

And I will make thee beds of roses
And a thousand fragrant posies,
A cap of flowers, and a kirtle
Embroidered all with leaves of myrtle;

A gown made of the finest wool
Which from our pretty lambs we pull;
Fair lined slippers for the cold,
With buckles of the purest gold;

A belt of straw and ivy buds,
With coral clasps and amber studs:
And if these pleasures may thee move,
Come live with me, and be my love.

The shepherds' swains shall dance and sing
For thy delight each May morning:
If these delights thy mind may move,
Then live with me and be my love.

Christopher Marlowe (1564–1593)

The business of the poet is not to find new emotions, but to use the ordinary ones and, in working them up into poetry, to express feelings which are not in actual emotions at all.

T S Eliot

Sonnet 18

Shall I compare thee to a summer's day?
Thou art more lovely and more temperate:
Rough winds do shake the darling buds of May,
And summer's lease hath all too short a date:
Sometimes too hot the eye of heaven shines,
And often is his gold complexion dimmed;
And every fair from fair sometimes declines,
By chance or nature's changing course untrimmed;
But thy eternal summer shall not fade,
Nor lose possession of that fair thou ow'st;
Nor shall death brag thou wander'st in his shade,
When in eternal lines to time thou grow'st;
So long as men can breathe, or eyes can see,
So long lives this, and this gives life to thee.

William Shakespeare (1564–1616)

A true sonnet goes eight lines and then takes a turn for better or worse and goes six or eight lines more.

Robert Frost

Sonnet 130

My mistress' eyes are nothing like the sun;
Coral is far more red than her lips' red;
If snow be white, why then her breasts are dun;
If hairs be wires, black wires grow on her head.
I have seen roses damasked, red and white,
But no such roses see I in her cheeks;
And in some perfumes is there more delight
Than in the breath that from my mistress reeks.
I love to hear her speak, yet well I know
That music hath a far more pleasing sound;
I grant I never saw a goddess go;
My mistress, when she walks, treads on the ground.
And yet, by heaven, I think my love as rare
As any she belied with false compare.

William Shakespeare (1564–1616)

The poet is a bird of strange moods. He descends from his lofty domain to tarry among us, singing; if we do not honour him he will unfold his wings and fly back to his dwelling place.

Kahlil Gibran

When Daisies Pied
(*from Love's Labour's Lost*)
Spring

When daisies pied and violets blue
  And ladysmocks all silver-white
And cuckoobuds of yellow hue
  Do paint the meadows with delight,
The cuckoo then, on every tree,
Mocks married men; for thus sings he,
          Cuckoo;
Cuckoo, cuckoo: Oh word of fear,
Unpleasing to a married ear!
When shepherds pipe on oaten straws,
  And merry larks are plowmen's clocks,
When turtles tread, and rooks, and daws,
  And maidens bleach their summer smocks,
The cuckoo then, on every tree,
Mocks married men; for thus sings he,
          Cuckoo;
Cuckoo, cuckoo: Oh word of fear,
Unpleasing to a married ear!

William Shakespeare (1564–1616)

The world is so great and rich, and life so full of variety, that you can never lack occasions for poems.

Johann Wolfgang von Goethe

Poetry should be great and unobtrusive, a thing which enters into one's soul, and does not startle it or amaze it with itself but with its subject.

John Keats

from **The Sun Rising**

Busy old fool, unruly sun,
Why dost thou thus,
Through windows and through curtains call on us?
Must to thy motions lovers' seasons run?
Saucy pedantic wretch, go chide
Late school boys and sour prentices,
Go tell court huntsmen that the king will ride,
Call country ants to harvest offices;
Love, all alike, no season knows nor clime,
Nor hours, days, months, which are the rags of time.

Thy beams, so reverend and strong
Why shouldst thou think?
I could eclipse and cloud them with a wink
But that I would not lose her sight so long;
If her eyes have not blinedd thine,
Look, and tomorrow late tell me,
Whether both th' Indias of spice and mine
Be where thou leftst them, or lie here with me.
Ask for those kings whom thou saw'st yesterday
And thou shalt hear, All here in one bed lay.

John Donne (1572–1631)

The forms of things unknown, the poet's pen
Turns them to shapes, and gives to airy nothing
A local habitation and a name.

William Shakespeare

A poet, any real poet, is simply an alchemist who transmutes his cynicism regarding human beings into an optimism regarding the moon, the stars, the heavens, and the flowers, to say nothing of Spring, love, and dogs.

George Jean Nathan

Song: To Celia

Drink to me only with thine eyes,
And I will pledge with mine;
Or leave a kiss but in the cup,
And I'll not look for wine.
The thirst that from the soul doth rise,
Doth ask a drink divine:
But might I of Jove's nectar sup,
I would not change for thine.

I sent thee late a rosy wreath,
Not so much honouring thee,
As giving it a hope, that there
It could not withered be.
But thou thereon did'st only breathe,
And sent'st it back to me;
Since when it grows and smells, I swear,
Not of itself, but thee.

Ben Jonson (1573–1637)

In poetry, you must love the words, the ideas and the images and rhythms with all your capacity to love anything at all.

Wallace Stevens

Delight in Disorder

A sweet disorder in the dress
Kindles in clothes a wantonness.
A lawn about the shoulders thrown
Into a fine distraction;
An erring lace, which here and there
Enthralls the crimson stomacher;
A cuff neglectful, and thereby
Ribbons to flow confusedly;
A winning wave, deserving note,
In the tempestuous petticoat;
A careless shoestring, in whose tie
I see a wild civility;
Do more bewitch me than when art
Is too precise in every part.

Robert Herrick (1591–1674)

To the Virgins, to Make Much of Time

Gather ye rosebuds while ye may,
   Old time is still a-flying;
And this same flower that smiles today
   Tomorrow will be dying.

The glorious lamp of heaven, the sun,
   The higher he's a-getting,
The sooner will his race be run,
   And nearer he's to setting.

That age is best which is the first,
   When youth and blood are warmer;
But being spent, the worse, and worst
   Times still succeed the former.

Then be not coy, but use your time,
   And, while ye may, go marry;
For, having lost but once your prime,
   You may forever tarry.

Robert Herrick (1591–1674)

A poet's pleasure is to withhold a little of his meaning, to intensify by mystification. He unzips the veil from beauty, but does not remove it.

E B White

When I Consider How My Light Is Spent

When I consider how my light is spent
  Ere half my days, in this dark world and wide,
  And that one talent which is death to hide
  Lodged with me useless, though my soul more bent
To serve therewith my Maker, and present
  My true account, lest he returning chide;
  "Doth God exact day-labour, light denied?"
  I fondly ask; but Patience to prevent
That murmur, soon replies, "God doth not need
  Either man's work or his own gifts; who best
  Bear his mild yoke, they serve him best. His state
Is kingly. Thousands at his bidding speed
  And post o'er land and ocean without rest:
  They also serve who only stand and wait."

John Milton (1608–1674)

Song

Why so pale and wan, fond lover?
  Prithee, why so pale?
Will, when looking well can't move her,
  Looking ill prevail?
  Prithee, why so pale?

Why so dull and mute, young sinner?
  Prithee, why so mute?
Will, when speaking well can't win her,
  Saying nothing do't?
  Prithee, why so mute?

Quit, quit, for shame; this will not move,
  This cannot take her.
If of herself she will not love,
  Nothing can make her:
  The devil take her!

Sir John Suckling (1609–1642)

All good poetry is forged slowly and patiently, link by link, with sweat and blood and tears.

Lord Alfred Douglas

from **To His Coy Mistress**

Had we but world enough, and time,
This coyness, lady, were no crime.
We would sit down, and think which way
To walk, and pass our long love's day.
Thou by the Indian Ganges' side
Shoudst rubies find; I by the tide
Of Humber would complain. I would
Love you ten years before the flood,
And you should, if you please, refuse
Till the conversion of the Jews.
My vegetable love should grow
Vaster than empires and more slow;
An hundred years should go to praise
Thine eyes, and on they forehead gaze;
Two hundred to adore each breast,
But thirty thousand to the rest;
An age at least to every part,
And the last age should show your heart.

Andrew Marvell (1621–1678)

A poem is made up of thoughts, each of which filled the whole sky of the poet in its turn.

Ralph Waldo Emerson

from **Auguries of Innocence**

To see a World in a Grain of Sand
And a Heaven in a Wild Flower
Hold Infinity in the palm of your hand
And Eternity in an hour
A Robin Red breast in a Cage
Puts all Heaven in a Rage
A dove house filld with doves and Pigeons
Shudders Hell thro all its regions
A dog starvd at his Masters Gate
Predicts the ruin of the State
A Horse misusd upon the Road
Calls to Heaven for Human blood
Each outcry of the hunted Hare
A fibre from the Brain does tear
A Skylark wounded in the wing
A Cherubim does cease to sing

William Blake (1757–1827)

from **The Tyger**

Tyger! Tyger! burning bright
In the forests of the night,
What immortal hand or eye
Could frame thy fearful symmetry?

In what distant deeps or skies
Burnt the fire of thine eyes?
On what wings dare he aspire?
What the hand, dare seize the fire?

And what shoulder, & what art,
Could twist the sinews of thy heart?
And when thy heart began to beat,
What dread hand? & what dread feet?

What the hammer? what the chain?
In what furnace was thy brain?
What the anvil? what dread grasp
Dare its deadly terrors clasp?

William Blake (1757–1827)

Poetry is the universal possession of mankind, revealing itself everywhere, and at all times, in hundreds and hundreds of men.

Johann Wolfgang von Goethe

from **To a Mouse**
On turning her up in her nest with
the plough, November, 1785

Wee, sleekit, cow'ring, tim'rous beastie,
O, what a panic's in thy breastie!
Thou need na start awa sae hasty,
        Wi' bickering brattle!
I wad be laith to rin an' chase thee,
        Wi' murd'ring pattle!

I'm truly sorry man's dominion
Has broken Nature's social union,
An' justifies that ill opinion
        Which makes thee startle
At me, thy poor earth-born companion,
        An' fellow mortal!

Robert Burns (1759–1796)

A Red, Red Rose

O my luve's like a red, red rose,
That's newly sprung in June;
O my luve's like the melodie
That's sweetly played in tune.

As fair art thou, my bonnie lass,
So deep in luve am I;
And I will luve thee still, my dear,
Till a' the seas gang dry.

Till a' the seas gang dry, my dear,
And the rocks melt wi' the sun:
O I will love thee still, my dear,
While the sands o' life shall run.

And fare thee weel, my only luve,
And fare thee weel awhile!
And I will come again, my luve,
Though it were ten thousand mile.

Robert Burns (1759–1796)

from **Tintern Abbey**

Lines composed a few miles above Tintern Abbey on revisiting the banks of the Wye during a tour. July 13, 1798.

Five years have passed; five summers, with the length
Of five long winters! and again I hear
These waters, rolling from their mountain-springs
With a soft inland murmur. Once again
Do I behold these steep and lofty cliffs,
That on a wild secluded scene impress
Thoughts of more deep seclusion; and connect
The landscape with the quiet of the sky.
The day is come when I again repose
Here, under this dark sycamore, and view
These plots of cottage ground, these orchard tufts,
Which at this season, with their unripe fruits,
Are clad in one green hue, and lose themselves
'Mid groves and copses. Once again I see
These hedgerows, hardly hedgerows, little lines
Of sportive wood run wild; these pastoral farms,
Green to the very door; and wreaths of smoke
Sent up, in silence, from among the trees!
With some uncertain notice, as might seem
Of vagrant dwellers in the houseless woods,
Or of some Hermit's cave, where by his fire
The Hermit sits alone.

William Wordsworth (1770–1850)

My Heart Leaps Up

My heart leaps up when I behold
  A rainbow in the sky:
So was it when my life began;
So is it now I am a man;
So be it when I shall grow old,
  Or let me die!
The Child is father of the Man;
And I could wish my days to be
Bound each to each by natural piety.

William Wordsworth (1770–1850)

from **I Wandered Lonely As a Cloud**

I wandered lonely as a cloud
That floats on high o'er vales and hills,
When all at once I saw a crowd,
A host, of golden daffodils;
Beside the lake, beneath the trees,
Fluttering and dancing in the breeze.

Continuous as the stars that shine
And twinkle on the milky way,
They stretched in never-ending line
Along the margin of a bay:
Ten thousand saw I at a glance,
Tossing their heads in sprightly dance.

William Wordsworth (1770–1850)

from **Kubla Khan**
Or a vision in a dream. A fragment.

In Xanadu did Kubla Khan
A stately pleasure dome decree:
Where Alph, the sacred river, ran
Through caverns measureless to man
  Down to a sunless sea.
So twice five miles of fertile ground
With walls and towers were girdled round:
And there were gardens bright with sinuous rills,
Where blossomed many an incense-bearing tree;
And here were forests ancient as the hills,
Enfolding sunny spots of greenery.

Samuel Taylor Coleridge (1772–1834)

She Walks in Beauty

She walks in beauty, like the night
  Of cloudless climes and starry skies;
And all that's best of dark and bright
  Meet in her aspect and her eyes:
Thus mellow'd to that tender light
  Which heaven to gaudy day denies.

One shade the more, one ray the less,
  Had half impair'd the nameless grace
Which waves in every raven tress,
  Or softly lightens o'er her face;
Where thoughts serenely sweet express
  How pure, how dear their dwelling-place.

And on that cheek, and o'er that brow,
  So soft, so calm, yet eloquent,
The smiles that win, the tints that glow,
  But tell of days in goodness spent,
A mind at peace with all below,
  A heart whose love is innocent!

Lord Byron (1788–1824)

A poet is a nightingale, who sits in darkness and sings to cheer its own solitude with sweet sounds.

Percy Bysshe Shelley

from **To a Skylark**

Hail to thee, blithe Spirit!
　　Bird thou never wert,
That from Heaven, or near it,
　　Pourest thy full heart
In profuse strains of unpremeditated art.

Higher still and higher
　　From the earth thou springest
Like a cloud of fire;
　　The blue deep thou wingest,
And singing still dost soar, and soaring ever singest.

In the golden lightning
　　Of the sunken sun,
O'er which clouds are bright'ning,
　　Thou dost float and run;
Like an unbodied joy whose race is just begun.

Percy Bysshe Shelley (1792–1822)

A good poem is a contribution to reality. The world is never the same once a good poem has been added to it. A good poem helps to change the shape and significance of the universe, helps to extend everyone's knowledge of himself and the world around him.

Dylan Thomas

from **Ode to a Nightingale**

My heart aches, and a drowsy numbness pains
   My sense, as though of hemlock I had drunk,
Or emptied some dull opiate to the drains
   One minute past, and Lethe-wards had sunk:
'Tis not through envy of thy happy lot,
   But being too happy in thine happiness —
      That thou, light-winged Dryad of the trees,
        In some melodious plot
   Of beechen green, and shadows numberless,
      Singest of summer in full-throated ease.

John Keats (1795–1821)

John Keats

All poets who, when reading from their own works, experience a choked feeling, are major.

E B White

from **Sonnets from the Portuguese**

How do I love thee? Let me count the ways.
I love thee to the depth and breadth and height
My soul can reach, when feeling out of sight
For the ends of Being and ideal Grace.
I love thee to the level of everyday's
Most quiet need, by sun and candle-light.
I love thee freely, as men strive for Right;
I love thee purely, as they turn from Praise.
I love thee with the passion put to use
In my old griefs, and with my childhood's faith.
I love thee with a love I seemed to lose
With my lost saints — I love thee with the breath,
Smiles, tears, of all my life! — and, if God choose,
I shall but love thee better after death.

Elizabeth Barrett Browning (1806–1861)

It is my heart that makes my songs, not I.

Sara Teasdale

Haiku

a swaying hunched
on horseback freezing
shadow

Haiku

alone but
the mosquitoes
won't let me be

from **The Children's Hour**

Between the dark and the daylight,
　When the night is beginning to lower,
Comes a pause in the day's occupations,
　That is known as the Children's Hour.

I hear in the chamber above me
　The patter of little feet,
The sound of a door that is opened,
　And voices soft and sweet.

From my study I see in the lamplight,
　Descending the broad hall stair,
Grave Alice, and laughing Allegra,
　And Edith with golden hair.

A whisper, and then a silence:
　Yet I know by their merry eyes
They are plotting and planning together
　To take me by surprise.

Henry Wadsworth Longfellow (1807–1882)

Not philosophy, after all, not humanity, just sheer joyous power of song, is the primal thing in poetry.

Max Beerbohm

from **The Raven**

Once upon a midnight dreary, while I pondered,
                                        weak and weary,
Over many a quaint and curious volume of
                                        forgotten lore —
While I nodded, nearly napping, suddenly there
                                        came a tapping,
As of some one gently rapping, rapping at my
                                        chamber door.
''Tis some visitor,' I muttered, 'tapping at my
                                        chamber door
                Only this and nothing more.'

Ah, distinctly I remember it was in the bleak
                                        December;
And each separate dying ember wrought its ghost
                                        upon the floor
Eagerly I wished the morrow; — vainly I had
                                        sought to borrow
From my books surcease of sorrow — sorrow for
                                        the lost Lenore —
                Nameless *here* for evermore.

Edgar Allan Poe (1809–1849)

All poetry is difficult to read,
The sense of it is, anyhow.

Robert Browning

from **Home-Thoughts, From Abroad**

Oh, to be in England
Now that April's there,
And whoever wakes in England
Sees, some morning, unaware,
That the lowest boughs and the brushwood sheaf
Round the elm-tree bole are in tiny leaf,
While the chaffinch sings on the orchard bough
In England — now!

Robert Browning (1812–1889)

from I Hear America Singing

I hear America singing, the varied carols I hear,
Those of mechanics, each one singing his as it should b
   blithe and strong,
The carpenter singing his as he measures his plank or
   beam,
The mason singing his as he makes ready for work, or
   leaves off work,
The boatman singing what belongs to him in his boat,
   the deck-hand singing on the steamboat deck,
The shoemaker singing as he sits on his bench, the hatte
   singing as he stands,
The wood-cutter's song, the ploughboy's on his way in
   the morning, or at noon intermission or at sundown,
The delicious singing of the mother, or of the young wi
   at work, or of the girl sewing or washing,
Each singing what belongs to him or her and to none
   else,
The day what belongs to the day — at night the party o
   young fellows, robust, friendly,
Singing with open mouths their strong melodious songs.

Walt Whitman (1819–1892)

Poetry is the impish attempt to paint the color of the wind.

Maxwell Bodenheim

from **When Lilacs Last in the Dooryard Bloom'd**

When lilacs last in the dooryard bloom'd,
And the great star early droop'd in the western sky
                                    in the night,
I mourn'd, and yet shall mourn with ever-returning
                                    spring.

Ever-returning spring, trinity sure to me you bring,
Lilac blooming perennial and drooping star in the
                                    west,
And thought of him I love.

O powerful western fallen star!
O shades of night — O moody, tearful night!
O great star disappear'd — O the black murk that
                                    hides the star!
O cruel hands that hold me powerless — O helpless
                                    soul of me!
O harsh surrounding cloud that will not free my soul.

Walt Whitman (1819–1892)

Prose, — words in their best order; poetry, — the best words in their best order.

Samuel Taylor Coleridge

from **Dover Beach**

The sea is calm tonight.
The tide is full, the moon lies fair
Upon the straits; on the French coast the light
Gleams and is gone; the cliffs of England stand,
Glimmering and vast, out in the tranquil bay.
Come to the window, sweet is the night-air!
Only, from the long line of spray
Where the sea meets the moon-blanched land,
Listen! you hear the grating roar
Of pebbles which the waves draw back, and fling,
At their return, up the high strand,
Begin, and cease, and then again begin,
With tremulous cadence slow, and bring
The eternal note of sadness in.

Matthew Arnold (1822–1888)

Poetry does not necessarily have to be beautiful to stick in the depths of our memory, there to occupy most mischievously the place doomed to invasion by certain melodies which, however blameworthy, can never be expunged.

Colette

I'm Nobody! Who Are You?

I'm nobody! Who are you?
Are you nobody, too?
Then there's a pair of us — don't tell!
They'd banish us, you know.

How dreary to be somebody!
How public, like a frog
To tell your name the livelong day
To an admiring bog!

Emily Dickinson (1830–1886)

have nothing to say and I am saying it and that is
poetry.

John Cage

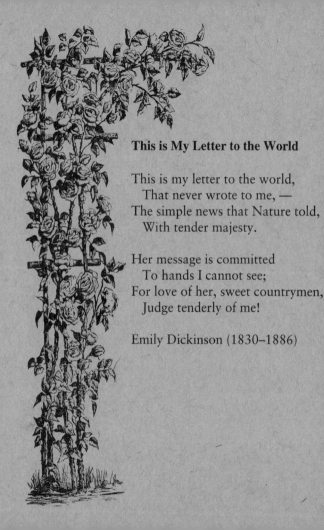

This is My Letter to the World

This is my letter to the world,
   That never wrote to me, —
The simple news that Nature told,
   With tender majesty.

Her message is committed
   To hands I cannot see;
For love of her, sweet countrymen,
   Judge tenderly of me!

Emily Dickinson (1830–1886)

Because I Could Not Stop for Death

Because I could not stop for Death,
He kindly stopped for me;
The carriage held but just ourselves
And Immortality.

We slowly drove, he knew no haste,
And I had put away
My labor, and my leisure too,
For his civility.

We passed the school where children played,
Their lessons scarcely done;
We passed the fields of gazing grain,
We passed the setting sun.

We paused before a house that seemed
A swelling of the ground;
The roof was scarcely visible,
The cornice but a mound.

Since then 'tis centuries; but each
Feels shorter than the day
I first surmised the horses' heads
Were toward eternity.

Emily Dickinson (1830–1886)

When you are describing
A shape, or sound, or tint;
Don't state the matter plainly,
But put it in a hint;
And learn to look at all things
With a sort of mental squint.

Lewis Carroll

Jabberwocky

'Twas brillig, and the slithy toves
   Did gyre and gimble in the wabe:
Al mimsy were the borogoves,
   And the mome raths outgrabe.

'Beware the Jabberwock, my son!
   The jaws that bite, the claws that catch!
Beware the Jubjub bird, and shun
   The frumious Bandersnatch!'

He took his vorpal sword in hand:
   Long time the manxome foe he sought —
So rested he by the Tumtum tree,
   And stood awhile in thought.

And, as in uffish thought he stood,
   The Jabberwock, with eyes of flame,
Came whiffling through the tulgey wood,
   And burbled as it came!

One, two! One, two! And through and through
   The vorpal blade went snicker-snack!
He left it dead, and with its head
   He went galumphing back.

And hast thou slain the Jabberwock?
  Come to my arms, my beamish boy!
O frabjous day! Callooh! Callay!'
  He chortled in his joy.

Twas brillig, and the slithy toves
  Did gyre and gimble in the wabe:
All mimsy were the borogoves,
  And the mome raths outgrabe.

Lewis Carroll (1832–1898)

Would you be a poet
Before you've been to school?
Ah, well! I hardly thought you
So absolute a fool

Lewis Carroll

Pied Beauty

Glory be to God for dappled things —
   For skies of couple-colour as a brinded cow;
      For rose-moles all in stipple upon trout that swim;
Fresh-firecoal chestnut-falls; finches' wings;
   Landscape plotted and pieced — fold, fallow, and
plough;
      And all trades, their gear and tackle and trim.

All things counter, original, spare, strange;
   Whatever is fickle, freckled (who knows how?)
      With swift, slow; sweet, sour; adazzle, dim;
He fathers-forth whose beauty is past change:
         Praise him.

Gerard Manley Hopkins (1844–1889)

If artists and poets are unhappy, it is after all because happiness does not interest them.

George Santayana

The courage of the poet is to keep ajar the door that leads into madness.

Christopher Morley

Haiku

opening the window
a window full
of spring

Santoka (1882–1940)

Poetry is what in a poem makes you laugh, cry, prickle, be silent, makes your toenails twinkle, makes you want to do this or that or nothing, makes you know that you are alone in the unknown world, that your bliss and suffering is forever shared and forever all your own.

Dylan Thomas

Haiku

working at it and
working at it and still
the tall grass grows

211

merciless indeed
under the ancient helmet
a cricket crickets

Basho (1644–1694)

The poet is the priest of the invisible.

Wallace Stevens

Haiku

with odour of plum
bursts the sunrise
mountain path

A great poet, a really great poet, is the most unpoetical of all creatures. But inferior poets are absolutely fascinating.

Oscar Wilde

A Birthday

My heart is like a singing bird
   Whose nest is in a water'd shoot;
My heart is like an apple-tree
   Whose boughs are bent with thick-set fruit;
My heart is like a rainbow shell
   That paddles in a halcyon sea;
My heart is gladder than all these,
   Because my love is come to me.

Raise me a daïs of silk and down;
   Hang it with vair and purple dyes;
Carve it in doves and pomegranates,
   And peacocks with a hundred eyes;
Work it in gold and silver grapes,
   In leaves and silver fleurs-de-lys;
Because the birthday of my life
   Is come, my love is come to me.

Christina Rossetti (1830–1894)

The Clod & the Pebble

"Love seeketh not Itself to please,
Nor for itself hath any care;
But for another gives its ease,
And builds a Heaven in Hells despair."

So sang a little Clod of Clay
Trodden with the cattle's feet;
But a Pebble of the brook,
Warbled out these metres meet:

"Love seeketh only Self to please,
To bind another to its delight,
Joys in another's loss of ease,
And builds a Hell in Heaven's despite."

William Blake (1757–1827)

When I Have Fears That I May Cease to Be

When I have fears that I may cease to be
  Before my pen has glean'd my teeming brain,
Before high-piled books, in charactery,
  Hold like rich garners the full ripen'd grain;
When I behold, upon the night's starr'd face,
  Huge cloudy symbols of a high romance,
And think that I may never live to trace
  Their shadows, with the magic hand of chance;
And when I feel, fair creature of an hour,
  That I shall never look upon thee more,
Never have relish in the faery power
  Of unreflecting love; — then on the shore
Of the wide world I stand alone, and think
Till love and fame to nothingness do sink.

John Keats (1795–1821)

Poetry is a counterfeit creation, and makes things that are not, as though they were.

John Donne

from **Ozymandias**

I met a traveler from an antique land
Who said: Two vast and trunkless legs of stone
Stand in the desert...Near them, on the sand,
Half sunk, a shattered visage lies, whose frown,
And wrinkled lip, and sneer of cold command,
Tell that its sculptor well those passions read
Which yet survive, stamped on these lifeless things,
The hand that mocked them, and the heart that fed:
And on the pedestal these words appear:
"My name is Ozymandias, king of kings:
Look on my works, ye Mighty, and despair!"

Percy Bysshe Shelley (1792–1822)

London

I wander thro' each charter'd street,
Near where the charter'd Thames does flow,
And mark in every face I meet
Marks of weakness, marks of woe.

In every cry of every Man,
In every Infant's cry of fear,
In every voice, in every ban,
The mind-forg'd manacles I hear.

How the Chimney-sweeper's cry
Every black'ning Church appalls;
And the hapless Soldier's sigh
Runs in blood down Palace walls.

But most thro' midnight streets I hear
How the youthful Harlot's curse
Blasts the new-born Infant's tear,
And blights with plagues the Marriage hearse.

William Blake (1757–1827)

The poet's mind is in fact a receptacle for seizing and storing up numberless feelings, phrases, images, which remain there until all the particles which can unite to form a new compound are present together.

T S Eliot

Hymn: Sung at the Completion of the Concord Monument

April 19, 1836

By the rude bridge that arched the flood,
   Their flag to April's breeze unfurled,
Here once the embattled farmers stood,
   And fired the shot heard round the world.

The foe long since in silence slept;
   Alike the conqueror silent sleeps;
And Time the ruined bridge has swept
   Down the dark stream which seaward creeps.

On this green bank, by this soft stream,
   We set to-day a votive stone;
That memory may their deed redeem,
   When, like our sires, our sons are gone.

Spirit, that made those heroes dare
   To die, or leave their children free,
Bid Time and Nature gently spare
   The shaft we raise to them and thee.

Ralph Waldo Emerson (1803–1882)

I have never started a poem yet whose end I knew.
Writing the poem is discovering.

Robert Frost

1755

To make a prairie it takes a clover and one bee,
One clover, and a bee,
And reverie.
The reverie alone will do,
If bees are few.

Emily Dickinson (1830–1886)

from **Barbara Frietchie**

Up from the meadows rich with corn,
Clear in the cool September morn,

The clustered spires of Frederick stand
Green-walled by the hills of Maryland.

Round about them orchards sweep,
Apple- and peach-tree fruited deep,

Fair as a garden of the Lord
To the eyes of the famished rebel horde,

On that pleasant morn of the early fall
When Lee marched over the mountain wall, —

Over the mountains winding down,
Horse and foot, into Frederick town.

Forty flags with their silver stars,
Forty flags with their crimson bars,

Flapped in the morning wind: the sun
Of noon looked down, and saw not one.

Up rose old Barbara Frietchie then,
Bowed with her fourscore years and ten;
Bravest of all in Frederick town,
She took up the flag the men hauled down;

In her attic-window the staff she set,
To show that one heart was loyal yet.

John Greenleaf Whittier (1807–1892)

from **Annabel Lee**

It was many and many a year ago,
                    In a kingdom by the sea,
That a maiden there lived whom you may know
                    By the name of Annabel Lee;
And this maiden she lived with no other thought
                    Than to love and be loved by me.

She was a child and *I* was a child,
                    In this kingdom by the sea,
But we loved with a love that was more than love –
                    I and my Annabel Lee –
With a love that the winged seraphs of Heaven
                    Coveted her and me.

And this was the reason that, long ago,
                    In this kingdom by the sea,
A wind blew out of a cloud by night
                    Chilling my Annabel Lee;
So that her highborn kinsmen came
                    And bore her away from me,
To shut her up in a sepulchre
                    In this kingdom by the sea.

Edgar Allan Poe (1809–1849)

1275

The Spider as an Artist
Has never been employed —
Though his surpassing Merit
Is freely certified

By every Broom and Bridget
Throughout a Christian Land —
Neglected Son of Genius
I take thee by the Hand —

Emily Dickinson (1830–1886)

Poetry makes its own pertinence, and a single stanza outweighs a book of prose.

Ralph Waldo Emerson

Maturing as a poet means maturing as the whole man, experiencing new emotions appropriate to one's age, and with the same intensity as the emotions of youth.

T S Eliot

A very good or very bad poet is remarkable; but a middling one who can bear?

Thomas Fuller

The poet should seize the Particular, and he should, if there be anything sound in it, thus represent the Universal.

Johann Wolfgang von Goethe

The Recall

I am the land of their fathers.
In me the virtue stays.
I will bring back my children,
After certain days.

Under their feet in the grasses
My clinging magic runs.
They shall return as strangers.
They shall remain as sons.

Over their heads in the branches
Of their new-bought, ancient trees,
I weave an incantation
And draw them to my knees.

Rudyard Kipling (1865–1936)

When you write in prose you say what you mean. When you write in rhyme you say what you must.

Oliver Wendell Holmes

Snowflakes

Out of the bosom of the Air,
  Out of the cloud-folds of her garments shaken,
Over the woodlands brown and bare,
  Over the harvest-fields forsaken,
    Silent, and soft, and slow
    Descends the snow.

Even as our cloudy fancies take
  Suddenly shape in some divine expression,
Even as the troubled heart doth make
  In the white countenance confession,
    The troubled sky reveals
    The grief it feels.

This is the poem of the air,
  Slowly in silent syllables recorded;
This is the secret of despair,
  Long in its cloudy bosom hoarded,
    Now whispered and revealed
    To wood and field.

Henry Wadsworth Longfellow (1807–1882)

A fine thought, to become poetry, must be seasoned in the upper warm garrets of the mind for long and long, then it must be brought down and slowly carved into words, shaped with emotion, polished with love.

David Grayson

It is not enough for poems to be fine; they must charm, and draw the mind of the listener at will.

Horace

Literature is a state of culture, poetry a state of grace, before and after culture.

Juan Ramón Jiménez

from **Song of Myself**

I celebrate myself, and sing myself,
And what I assume you shall assume,
For every atom belonging to me as good belongs to you.

I loaf and invite my soul,
I lean and loaf,at my ease observing a spear of summer
grass.

My tongue, every atom of my blood, formed from this
soil,
                         this air,
Born here of parents born here from parents the same,
and
                             their parents the same,
I, now thirty-seven years old in perfect health begin,
Hoping to cease not till death.

Creeds and schools in abeyance,
Retiring back a while suffced at what they are, but never
                             forgotten,
I harbor for good or bad, I permit to speak at every
hazard,
Nature without check with original energy.

Walt Whitman (1819–1892)

When power leads man toward arrogance, poetry reminds him of his limitations. When power narrows the areas of man's concern, poetry reminds him of the richness and diversity of his existence. When power corrupts, poetry cleanses.

John F Kennedy

As to the pure mind all things are pure, so to the poetic mind all things are poetical.

Henry Wadsworth Longfellow

The crown of literature is poetry. It is its end and aim. It is the sublimest activity of the human mind. It is the achievement of beauty and delicacy. The writer of prose can only step aside when the poet passes.

W Somerset Maugham

Poetry is the opening and closing of a door, leaving those who look through to guess about what is seen during a moment.

Carl Sandburg

Published by MQ Publications Limited
254-258 Goswell Road, London EC1V 7EB

Copyright © MQ Publications Limited
Reprinted 1997

Front cover illustration © Gordon Parker 1996

ISBN: 1 897954 65 4

Printed and bound in China